"There is beauty everywhere on the express condition that there is an eye capable of recognizing it."[1]

Jacques Kerchache

The Hand of Nature Butterflies, Beetles and Dragonflies

Fondation Cartier pour l'art contemporain

Thames & Hudson

For thousands o

ears, in every civilization, man has been attentive

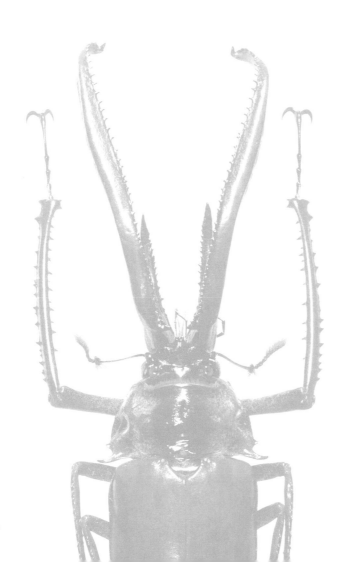

to his environment. Precious substances and forms, in particular, have always caught his eye.

Spurred on by the great voyagers and navigators, the Renaissance saw the emergence of curio rooms in which plants, minerals, fauna, flora, fossils, skulls, shells and insects were classified and arranged.

These "wonder rooms" kept pace with the latest discoveries, and the collections, arranged in methodical fashion, were presented in display cases or drawers.

In this context the notion of aesthetics could be said to apply more to the space represented by the curio room as such than to the objects themselves, all heterogeneous and chosen not for their plastic qualities but for their scarcity or singularity.

It wasn't until the Enlightenment and the Encyclopedists that methodical catalogues and inventories were rigorously established.

In the late nineteenth century, Jean-Henri Fabre became
a passionate spokesman for this microcosm with its hidden beauties. The plastic
qualities of the specimens he scrupulously examined did not escape him:
"Sometimes splendours are encountered that the imagination of a lapidary
would not dare conceive."[2]
And he goes even further by affirming:
"However rich a painter's palette might be, it will always be inferior to that of
realities. Neither will the sculptor's chisel ever exhaust the treasures
of natural modelling. Form and colour, beauty of contours and plays of light are
taught by the spectacle of things."[3]
It is no surprise, then, that this whimsical-looking entomologist should have
aroused the curiosity and interest of the Surrealists.
André Breton collected boxes of butterflies. In his apartment on the rue
de Fontaine in Paris, five boxes were hung on the wall amid the objects he loved.
But already in a photo dating from circa 1927, in the studio he shared with
his wife Simone, one can clearly make out a box placed prominently between
African and South Sea Islands' masks and a cubist-period Braque.
It is a parallel that Ernst Jünger had also sensed. In *Chasses subtiles* in 1967
he wrote, apropos a cetonia:

"That yellow should be concealed in this heavy, oily brown is perfectly comprehensible, after all; what is surprising is the abrupt jump by which it becomes clear. Had a painter risked this, Braque, for example, whose palette includes this mysterious brown, it would have been a stroke of genius."[4]

How, indeed, can one fail to be disturbed by the infinite perfection of these insects which partake at once of architecture, sculpture and painting and which give us the impression, as Jünger himself says, "of dealing with masterpieces, not of nature but of the human hand"?[5]

Following, no doubt, the long conversations he had with Breton, formative exchanges in terms of the gaze, Claude Lévi-Strauss has likewise noticed the analogy between art created by man and these wonders of nature:

"A bird, a beetle, a butterfly call for the same rapt contemplation that we reserve for a Tintoretto or a Rembrandt."[6]

Artists, for their part, have always been fascinated by these scholarly shambles, from which they have extracted the very substance by transforming specimens of a scientific nature or judged "bizarre" into works of art.

My critical path is itself that, not of a scientist or a collector, but of an art-lover whose vocabulary of signs has been forged and strengthened by all cultures and eras without discrimination. I look at an insect as the work of a fully-fledged artist, bearer of a a specific identity. From the midst of a group I eliminate the commonplace to preserve the excellent. And when the eye comes to rest on a masterpiece, to aesthetic delight is added a strange sensation, as though something was eluding us, transcending us. Why not allow one's emotion to well up at this point, along with that sense of mystery, with neither rules nor constraints, from which poetry emerges?

Jacques Kerchache, May 1998

1. Translated from: Jean-Henri Fabre, *Souvenirs entomologiques*, Éditions Robert Laffont, Paris, 1989, vol. 1, p. 960

2. *Op cit.*, vol. 2, p. 58

3. *Op cit.*, vol 2, p. 103

4. Translated from: Ernst Jünger, *Chasses subtiles*, [Subtile Jagden], Christian Bourgois éditeur, Paris, 1993, p. 435

5. *Op cit.*, p. 42

6. Translated from: Claude Lévi-Strauss and Didier Éribon, *De Près et de loin: entretiens*, Points Seuil, Paris, 1996, p. 241

Ettore Sottsass
How

Beautiful!

The epiphany we call nature, namely that gigantic (for us) ball of rocks, sand, water, fire and gas that revolves dumbly in the dreadful silence of the cosmic void, inhabited by leaves, trees and various combinations of living cells that we call animals (including Australopithecus)—that ball, that nature, is not so gentle with the species now described as Homo Sapiens.

That ball isn't interested in the least in our existence; its power, heat, glaciers, winds, tremors, fragility, whims are not conceived for "sapient beings."

The responsibility to live, to survive—if we truly want to survive—the celestial ball leaves it all up to us, and that's it.

In order to survive in so-called nature, Homo Sapiens has always encountered more problems than solutions. Nature never proposes solutions, it doesn't even acknowledge the word "solution," it has no concern for solutions. Nature is what it is, where it is. For whom should it find solutions? The cosmos is mute.

If Homo Sapiens needs solutions, it has to find them, to invent them on its own and for itself. Why, then, do we keep feeling so keen about that deadly event, about that always oversized dimension we call the presence of nature?

Why do we look at an immense, inaccessible, deadly, iced mountain and say: "How beautiful!"?

Why do we look at a Tahitian sunset and say: "How beautiful!"—if the flaming sky holds the sign of the end of another day, a day now subtracted from our lives?

Why do we look at a young girl and say: "How beautiful!"—if we already know that on her face, that beauty endures only the moment we see it.

Why do we look at the green mamba—a smooth snake of the most lovely, phosphorescent, spring green color, hidden silently amid the forest leaves—perhaps the most poisonous snake on earth—and say: "How beautiful!"?

My beloved African song says: "C'est difficile l'amour" and then continues… "C'est pas facile la vie."
"C'est pas facile l'amour… c'est difficile la vie…"
This story of life not being easy is understood early on, very early on, perhaps even Australopithecus began to understand it.

What we still don't understand is why we "sapient beings" keep feeling so enthusiastic about an event as obscure as nature, about that permanent unknown, about that permanent question we continue to ask, knowing there's no answer.
Is it perhaps because that event is obscure? Or precisely because no matter how many questions we imagine, we never find answers? Are we perhaps hypnotized by the cosmic silence?
Do we perhaps equate beauty with obscurity? With silence? Do we perhaps equate beauty with that darkness where we lose all direction, all awareness, all connection? Where we lose all reference, all natural support? Where the human "substance"—which we have cherished for so long and for so long sought to define—loses sense, obliterated as it is in total obscurity? In total silence? In total perplexity?

When I was seven eight years old, my parents sent me to spend the summer with my grandparents, in Innsbruck. Every morning I swam in the green-brown waters of an icy pool; the pond lay amid meadows and birch-woods, on a sort of plateau at the foot of an enormous mountain.
To get to that pond I had to hike for perhaps an hour or more, through dense woods filled with fir trees, larch and pine, ancient, gloomy woods, lit by the occasional shaft of light. There were also raspberry bushes, also red and black bilberry plants, and sometimes also hidden mushrooms, yellow or red or brown…
At that time I was living in a state of complete nothingness, I understood nothing, I didn't think, I didn't know, I didn't ask questions. I was a combination of living cells. I was also bored, walking slowly on the soft, humid ground, decayed with centuries of fallen leaves. Here and there I gave a kick, out of boredom, out of solitude.

When I expected it least, a hesitant butterfly might happen to cross the forest shade, suddenly lit, for a moment, by a ray of sunlight; flying here and there noiselessly, who-knows-where it was going? And I immediately fell in love, immediately, desperately, with that secret apparition coming from who-knows-where to keep me company. I was no longer alone. I too would have liked to go with it. I would have liked to enter into the apparition. I too would have liked to be a secret apparition. Perhaps I would have liked to exist, no longer as a child, but as an apparition with no meaning. What this, maybe, the only way to be happy?

Those butterflies were small, pitiful little butterflies, ordinary butterflies, and they seemed to be in a hurry, they seemed to be a bit desperate. I remember they were a faded blue color. Still, they were in front of me, they appeared and brought me out of that sort of non-existence. They allowed me to feel part, some part, of the billions of existences of all forms, all combinations, all colors, all densities, all sounds, all brilliances, all movements, all odors, all brevities, all immensities, all births and all deaths, which—I understood later—are everything we call the universe, nature.

When an ordinary butterfly, light blue, nothing more, maybe with a little white edge around the wings, passed through the dark air of the woods—I remember—I opened my eyes wide and thought: "How beautiful!"

Perhaps, without my knowing it, was beauty all that is dark, secret and swift in nature's apparitions? Can I say that in those woods, with that anxious butterfly, I fell into a state of aesthetic ecstasy?

Then, during those distant summers, the woods gradually grew wider, their boundaries grew more and more distant and it took ever longer to pass through…

I realized that the woods were inhabited by other sudden apparitions, glittering as the stars falling from the sky: small flying animals, small hopping animals, small animals, plodding amid the decaying leaves on the ground, small motionless animals, hugging the bark of trees, small animals coupling, to produce other small, even smaller animals; small dying animals, small dead animals emptied out, dried up forever…

I realized that the shade of the woods was more and more inhabited by numberless apparitions and I — non-sense—was letting myself go; I was expanding, expanding into that infinite non-sense, into that infinite swarm of instantaneous apparitions without time into that endless show of colors and darkness, lustre and roughness, chrome and hair, transparencies and opacities, weight and lightness, length and shortness, straight lines and curves, speed and slowness, rush and calm, fears and outbursts…
The perfumed darkness of that forest was the scene of a ceaseless parade of unpredicable events, explosive events, unforeseen combinations, unattainable logic; and there, within it all, I disappeared.
In the midst of all those apparitions, it certainly didn't occur to me to ask questions. There was nothing more to explain, nothing more to judge, nothing more of nothing. I no longer felt as a separate entity, different from nature. I no longer felt "against" nature. I was no longer afraid. I only had my eyes open, wide open, gaping and cast headlong into a total state of ecstasy; cast headlong into one of those ecstasies where, for any reason, one is transported beyond the speed of light, deep into the cosmos, where one then vanishes; simply vanishes because one becomes—is—cosmos…

To be flung headlong into darkness, into the unknown, into secrecy, to the point where the secret is no longer secret, I mean to the point that it no longer occurs to you to "examine" the secret—this is perhaps the maximum aesthetic experience, the maximum aesthetic orgasm.
I tumbled into that orgasm, walking in those distant woods, when I found myself surrounded by a myriad, a myriad of small lights that arrived in silence from the secret cosmos.

January 2000

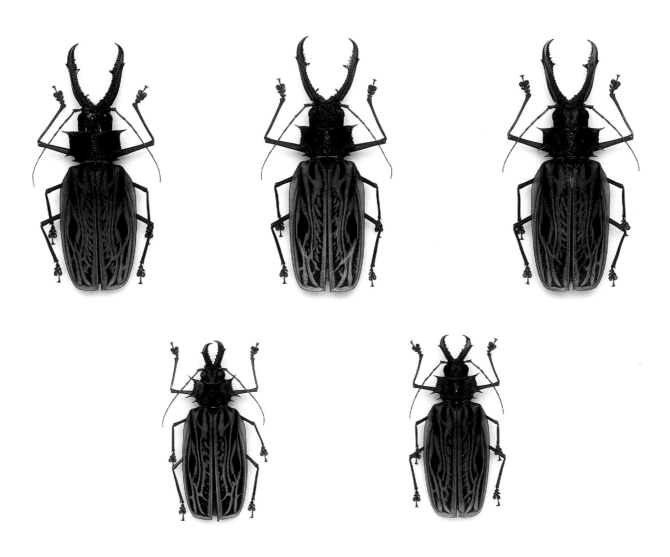

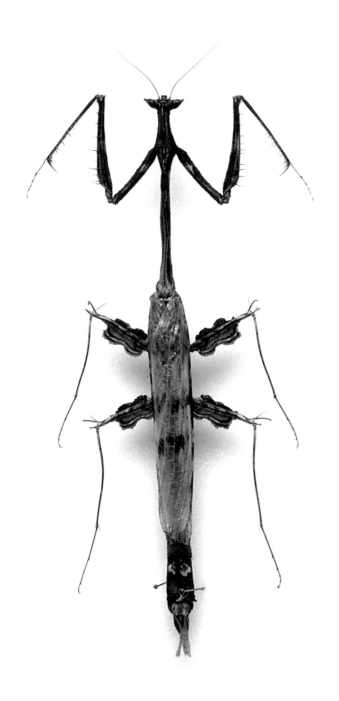

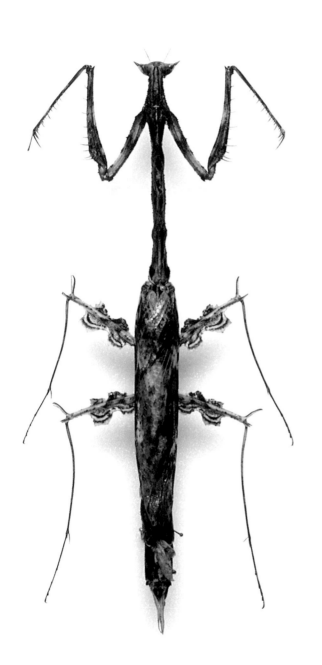

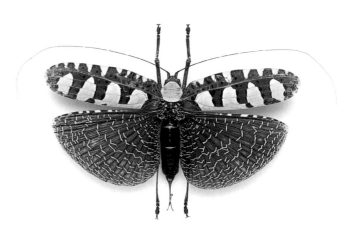

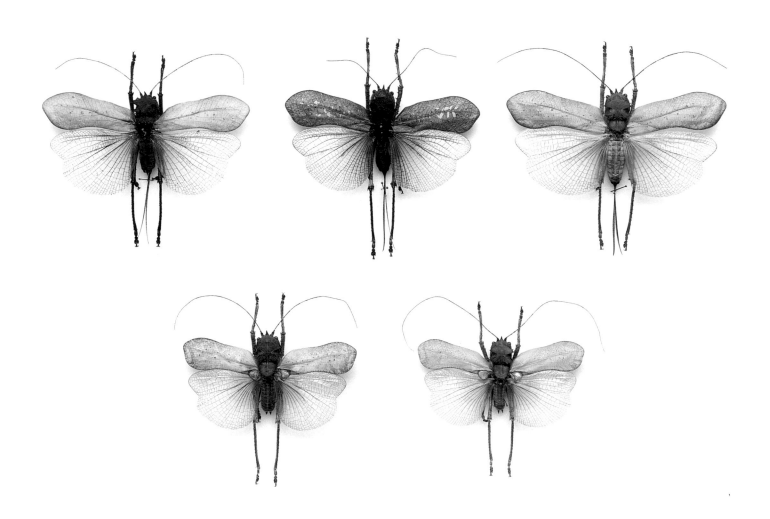

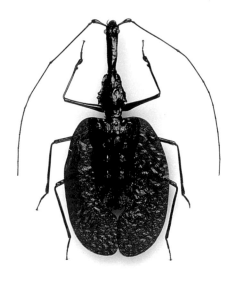
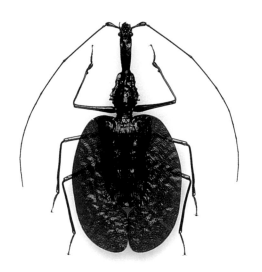
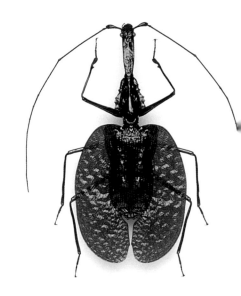
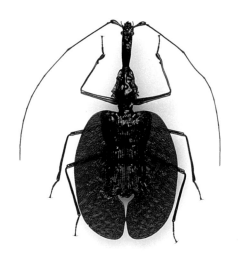
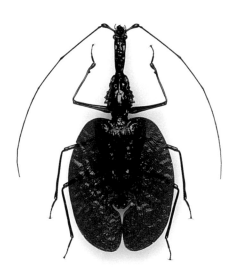
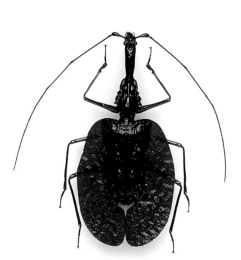

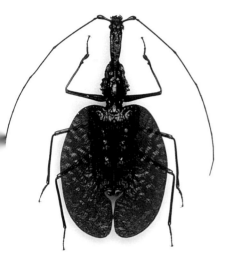

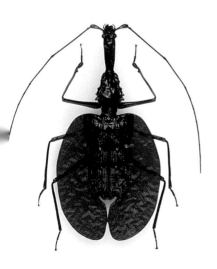

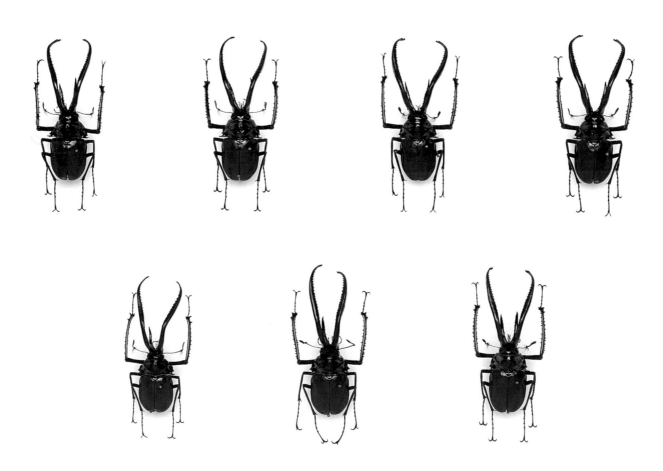

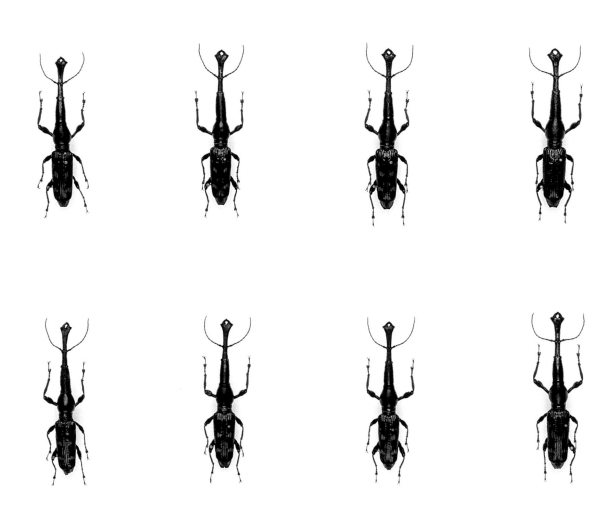

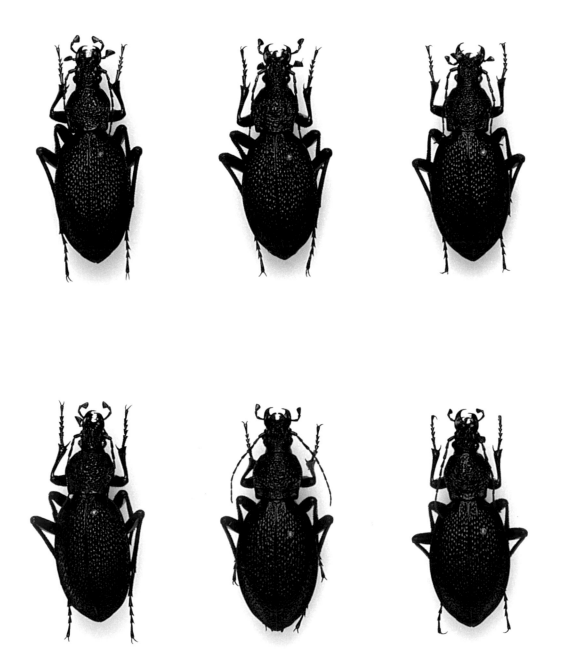

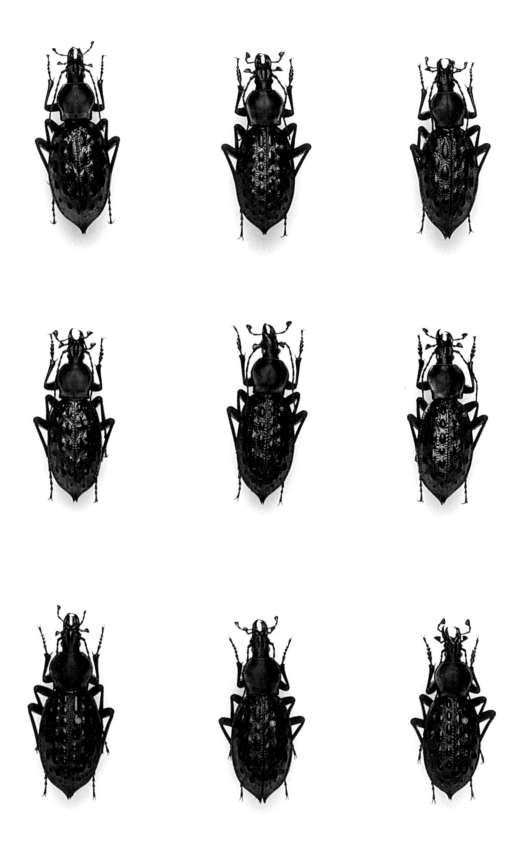

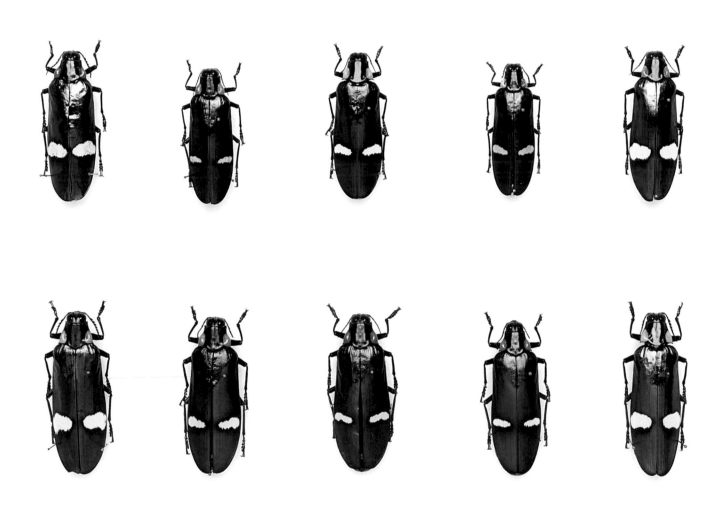

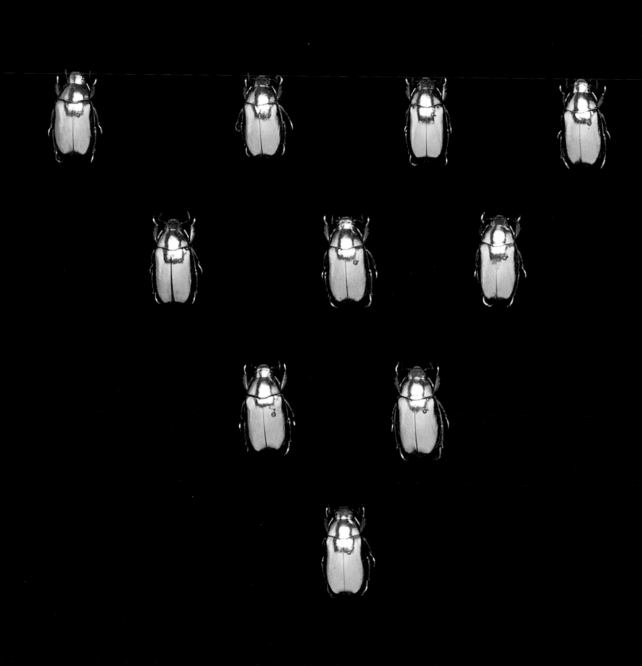

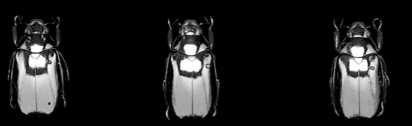

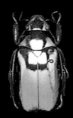
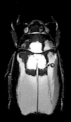

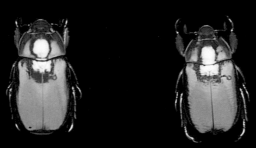

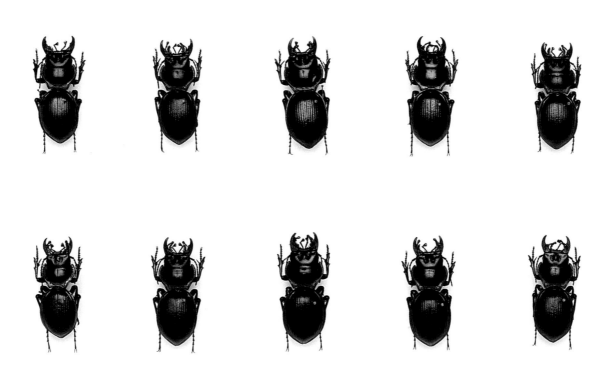

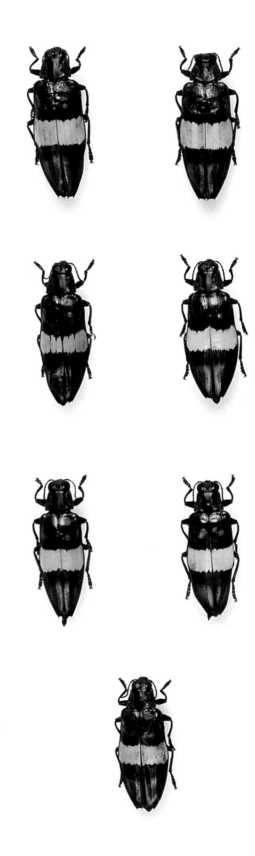

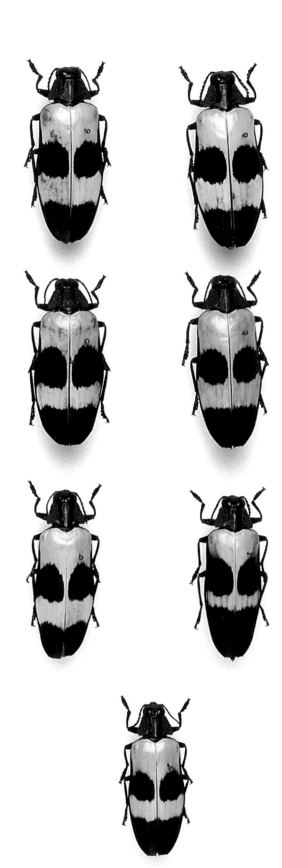

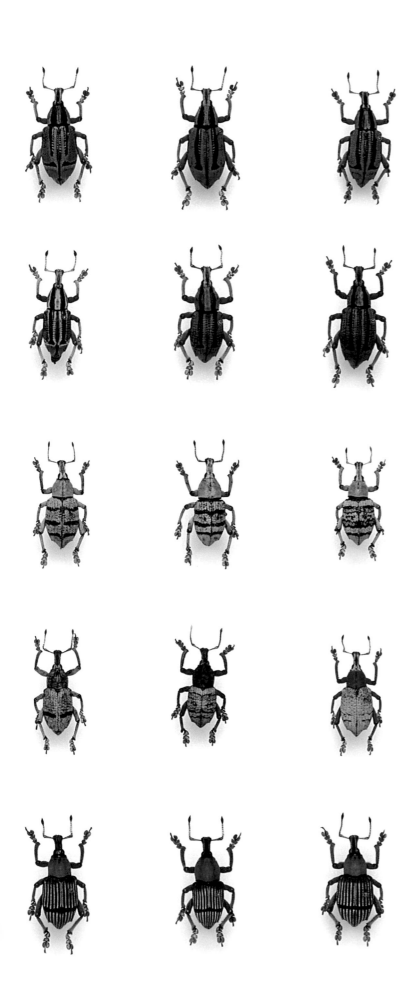

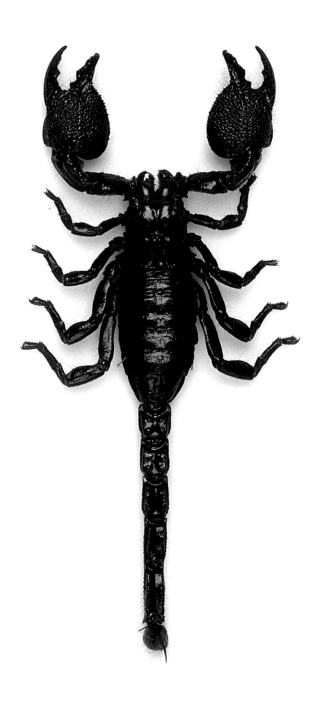

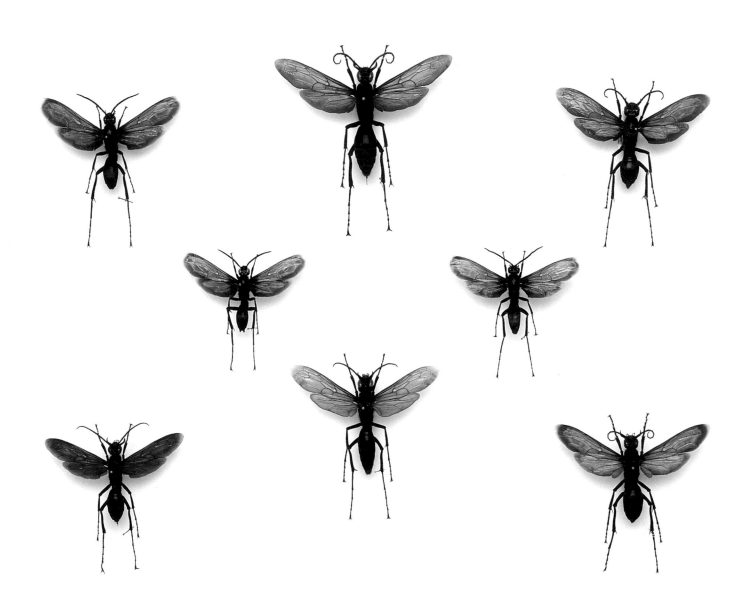

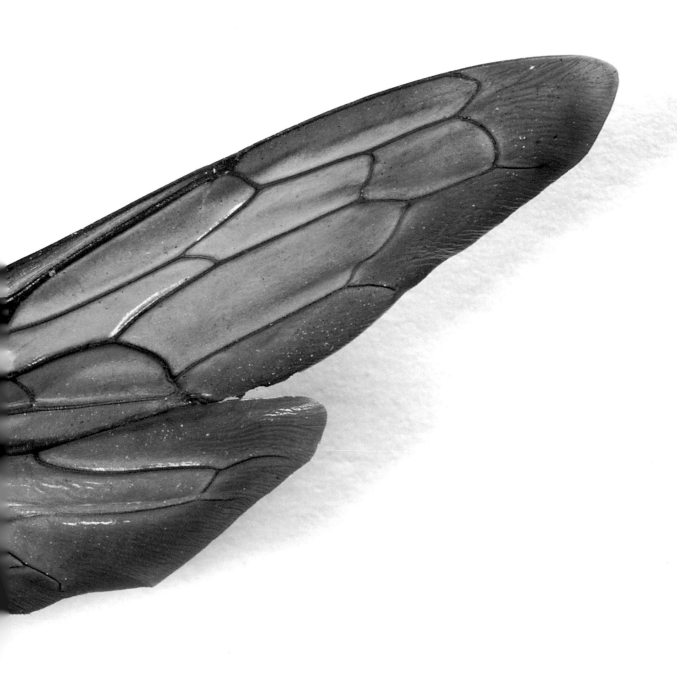

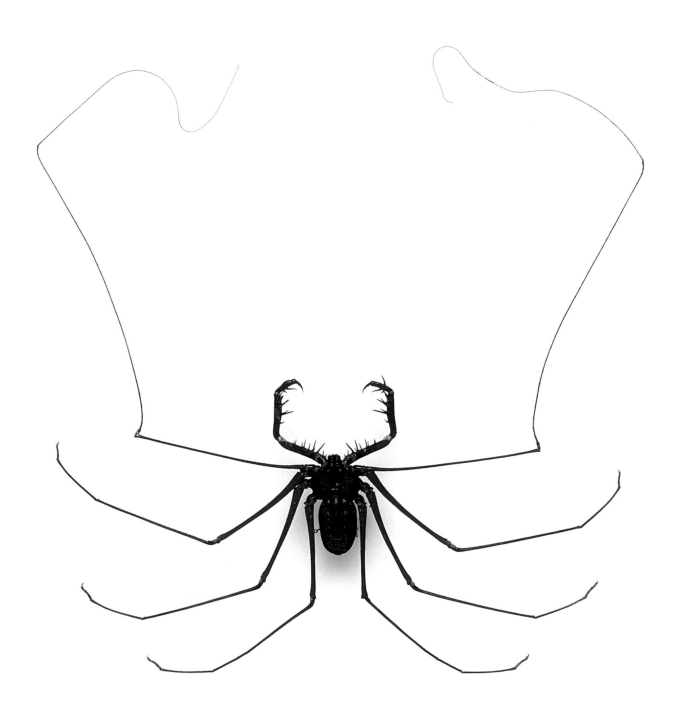

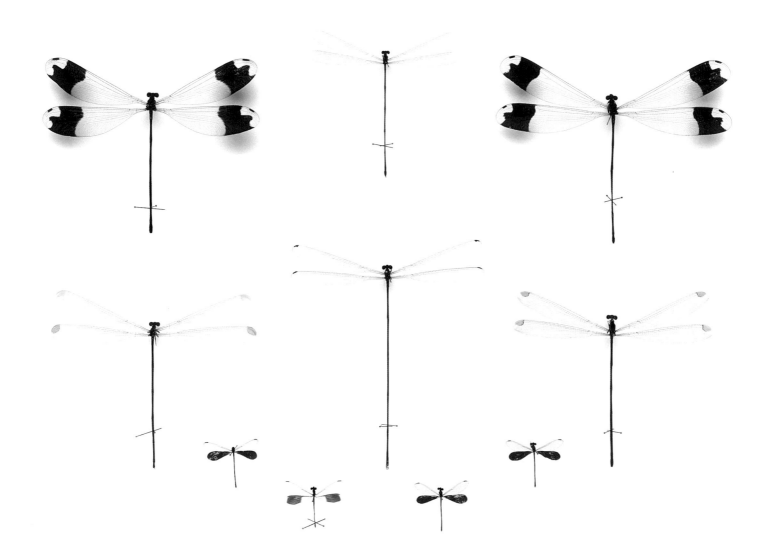

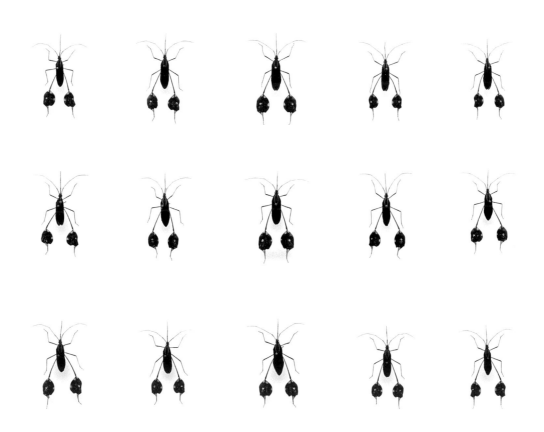

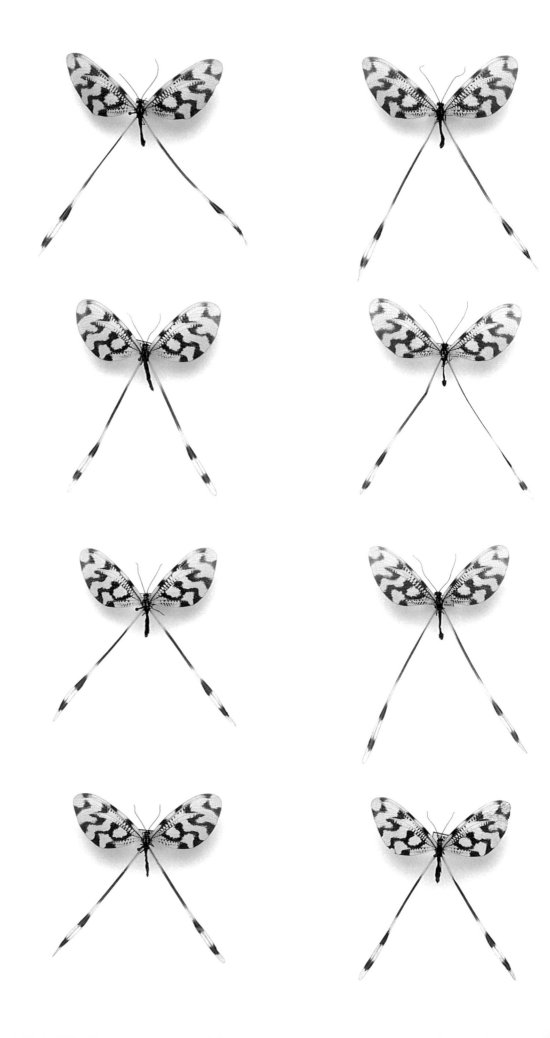

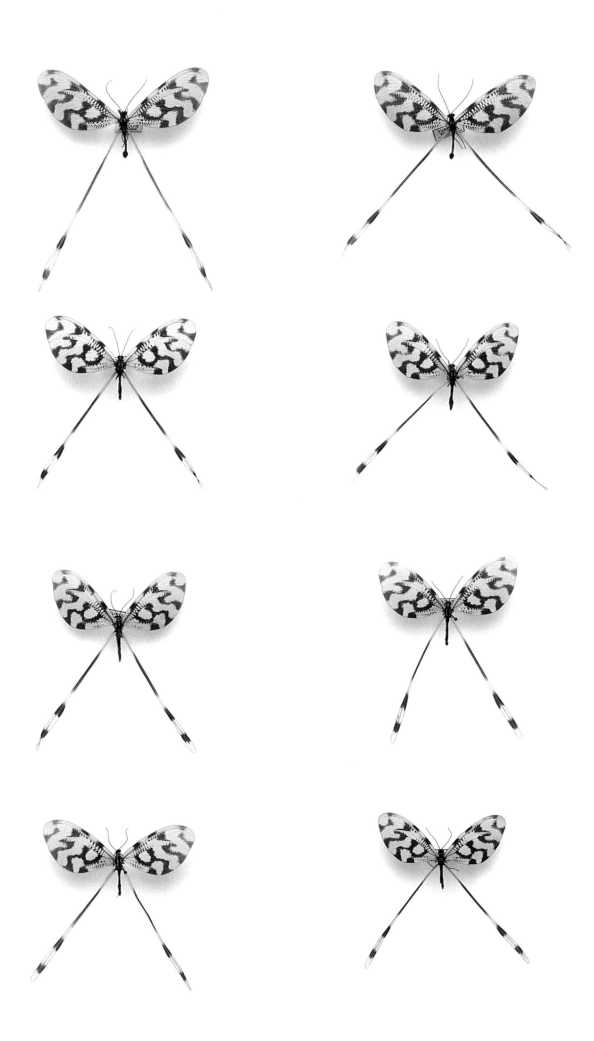

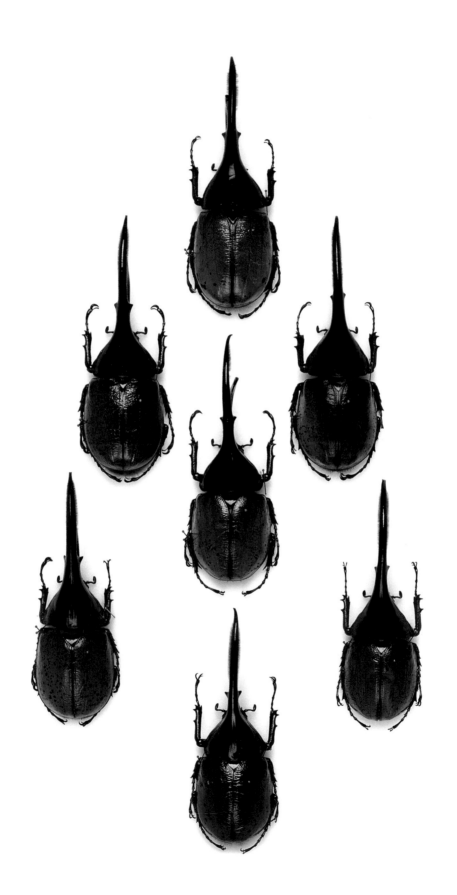

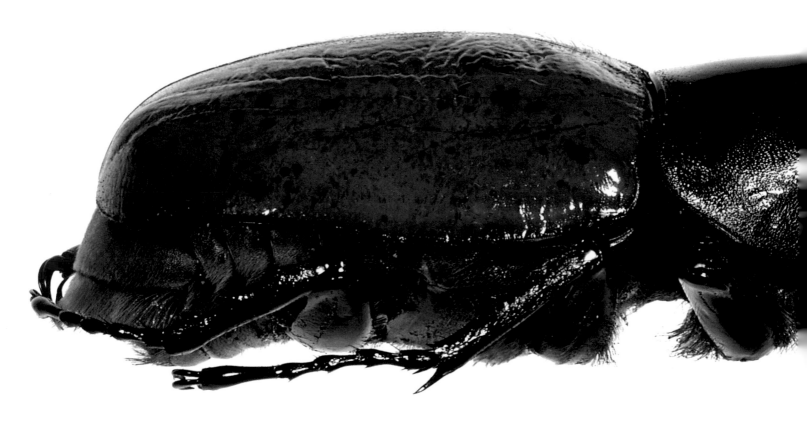

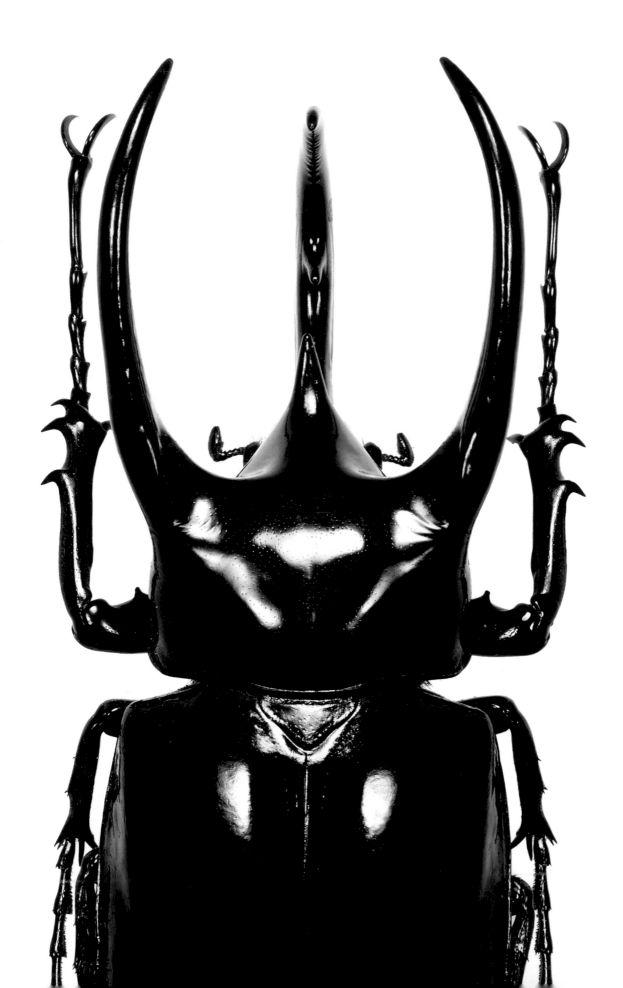

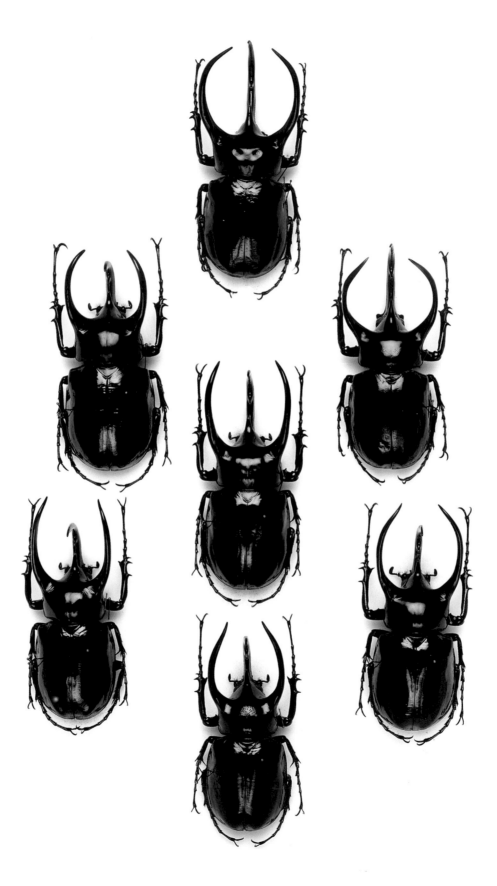

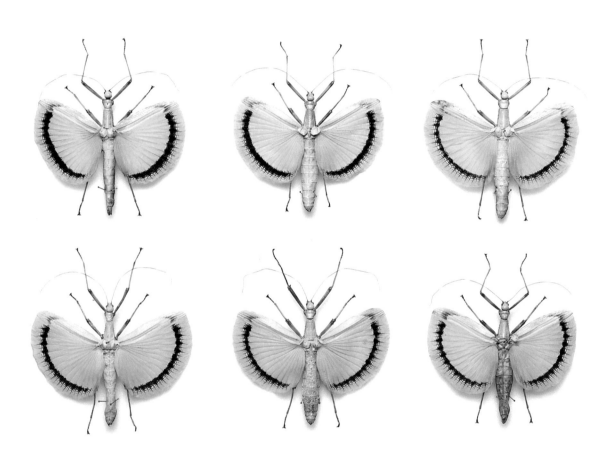

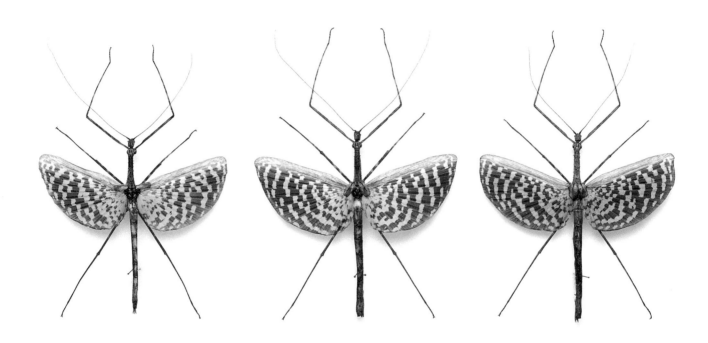

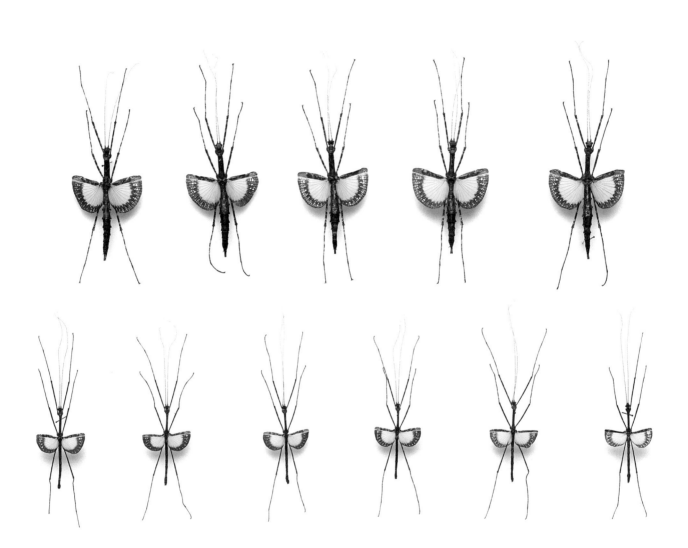

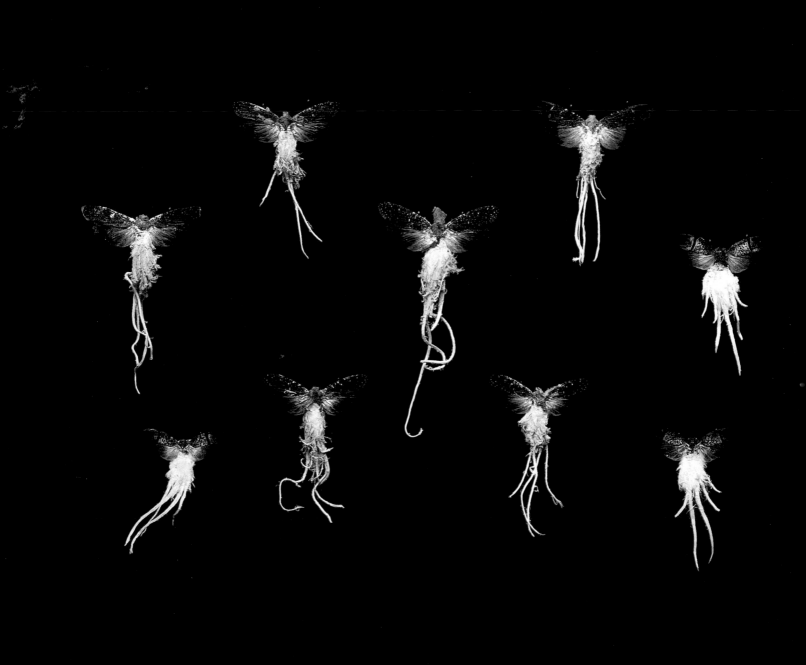

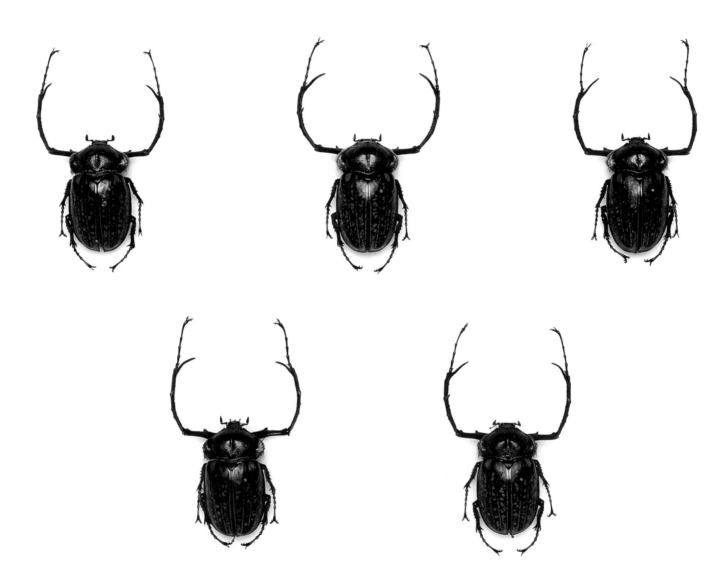

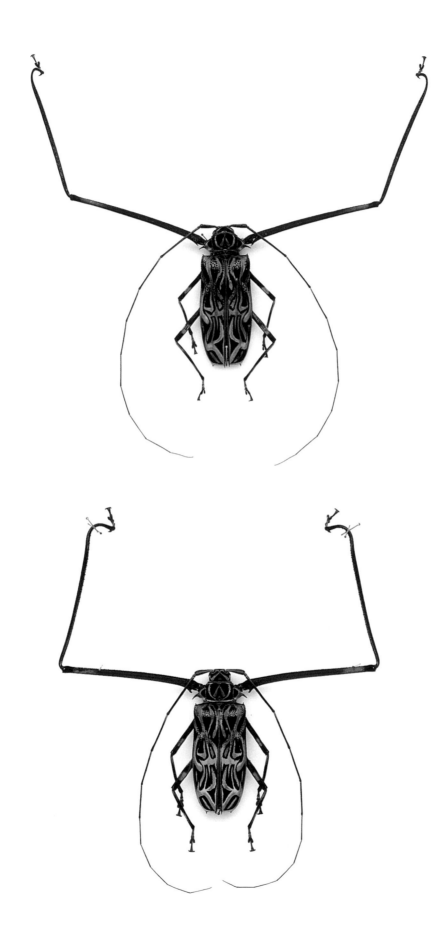

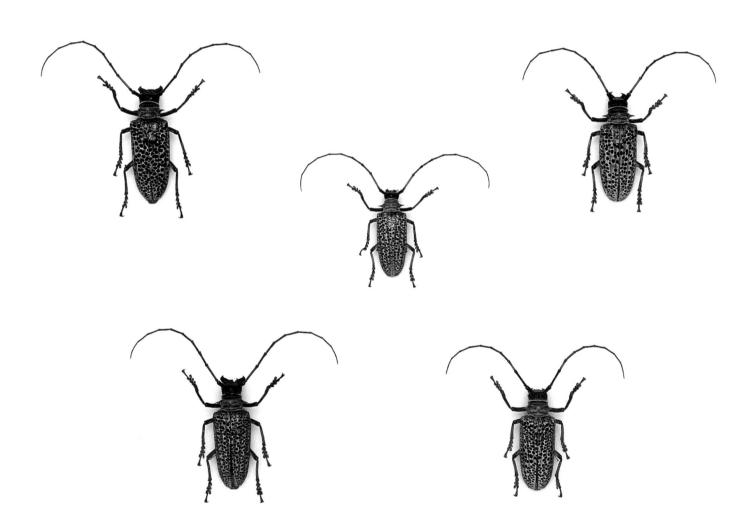

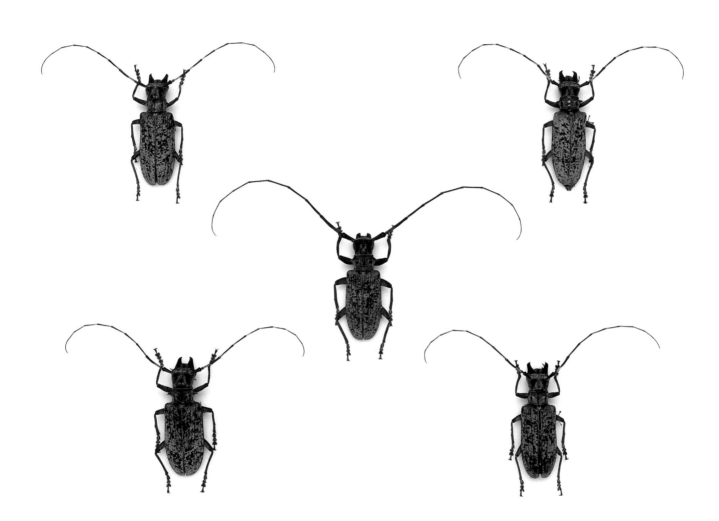

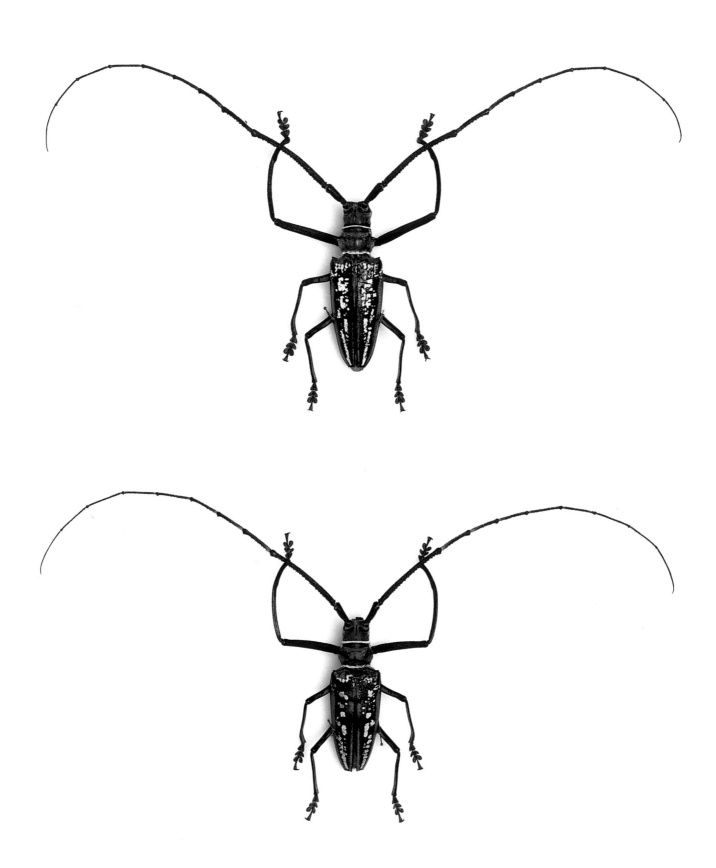

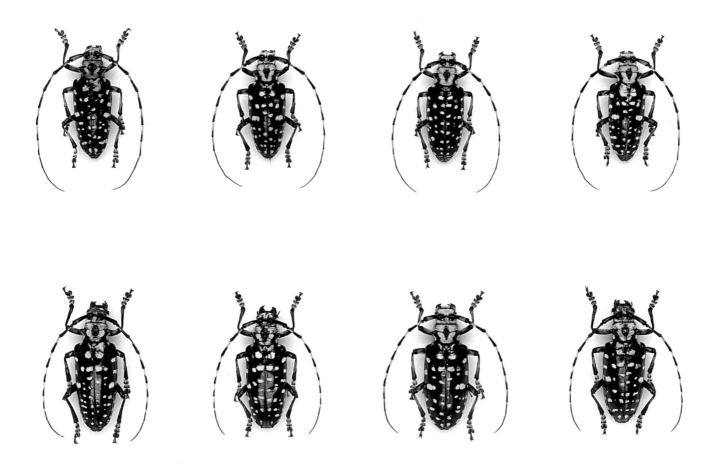

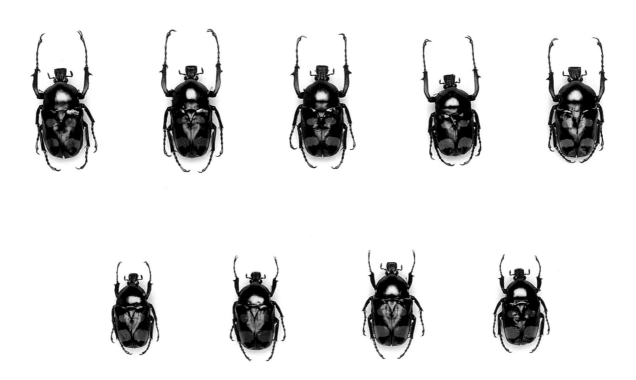

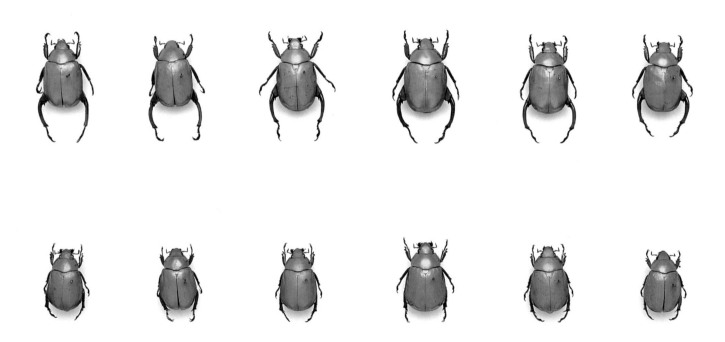

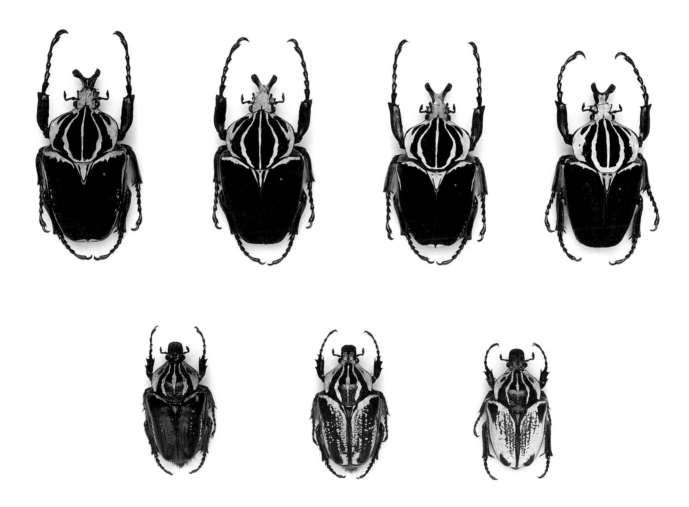

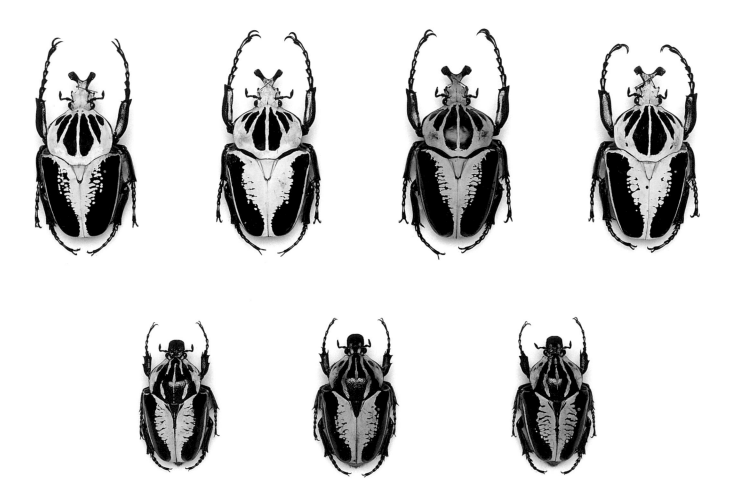

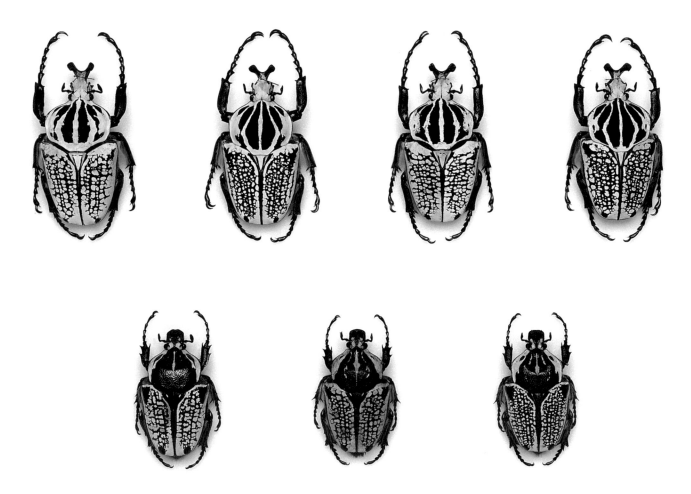

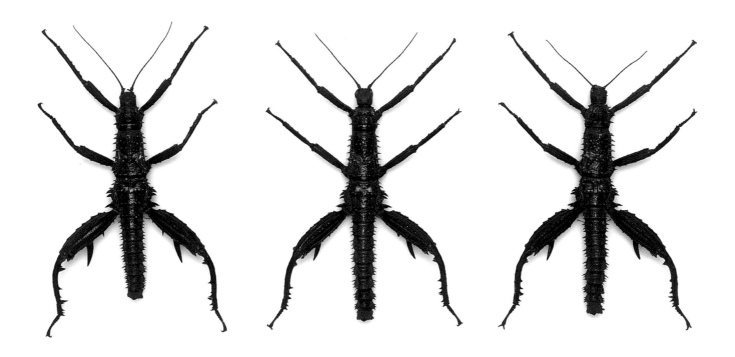

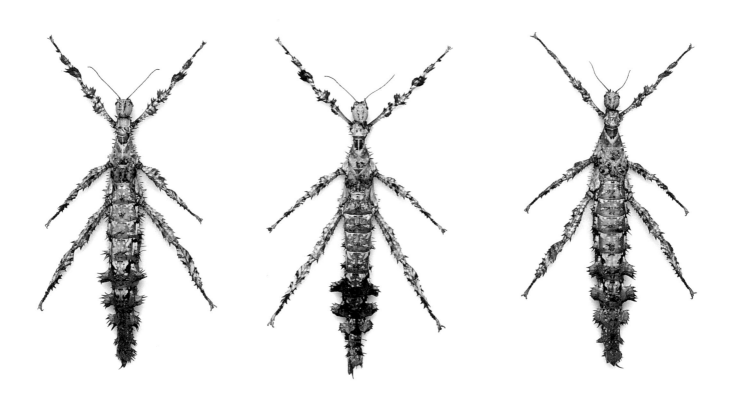

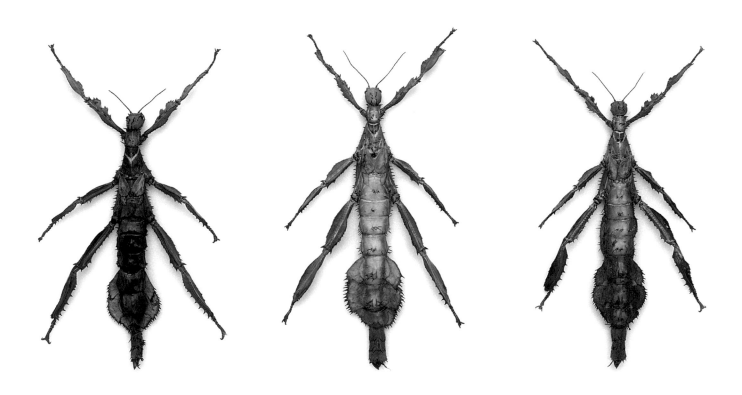

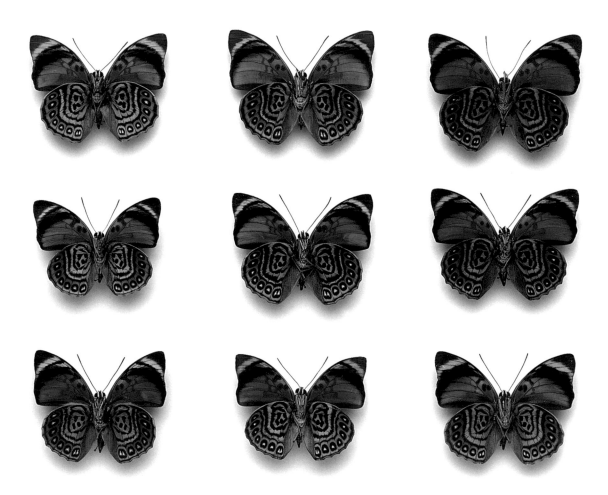

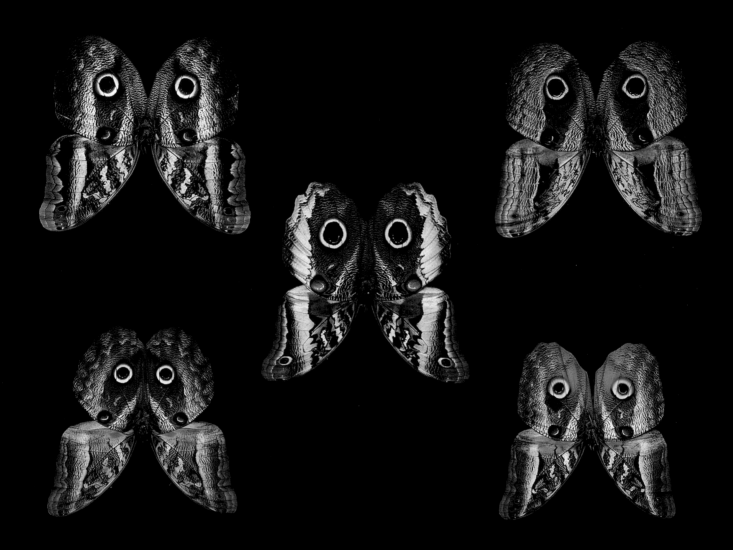

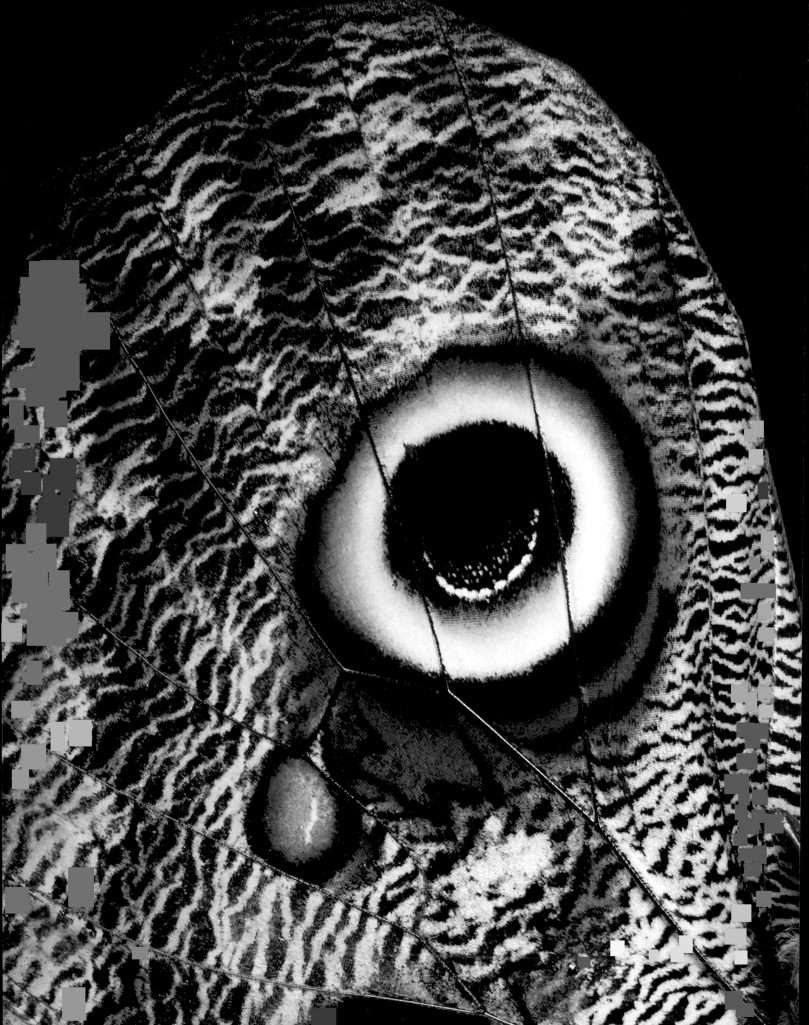

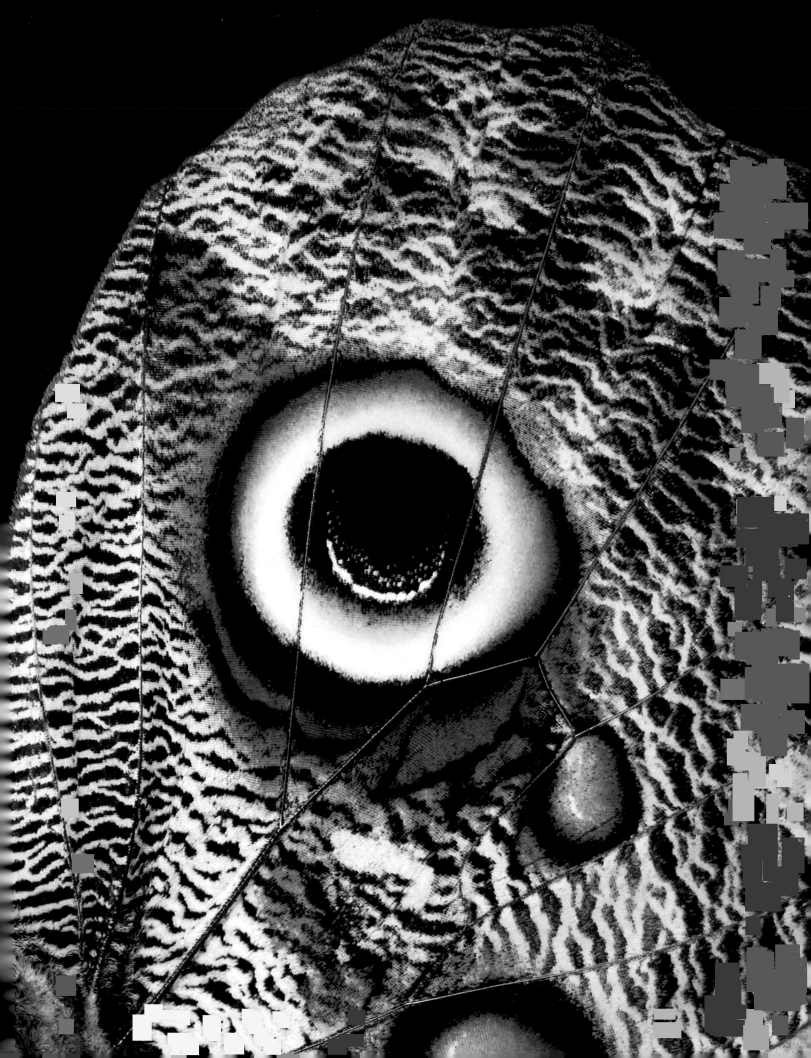

eurycnema goliath   cyphocrania gigas

sana imperialis   tanusia   acridoxena   siliquofera grandis

chiasognathus granti   eutrachelus temminck

plusiotis : resplendens/optima/argenteola/aurigans   mouhotia planipennis

eupholus   sagra buqueti   chrysophora chrysochlora

odonates   anisocelis   nemoptera sinuata

chalcosoma caucasus   megasoma elephas   phasmes   phasmes

fulgora lampetis   cheirotonus arnaud

pseudomeges marmoratus   petrognatha gigas   batocera wallace

chrysina macropus   goliathus goliatus

horricantha horrida   extatosoma popoi horridus   extatosoma

agrias sardana palus   agrias : beata/phalcido

thecla coronata   helicopi

macrodontia cervicornis   toxodera

phyllium giganteum   mormolyce phyllodes

coptolabrus ignigena/procrustes scabrosus   megaloxantha bicolor

sternocera pulchra   calodema ribbei/chrysochroa

ethocerus maximus   pandinus imperator   pepsis   phryne

phanaeus ensifer   dynastes hercules lichyi

phasmes   phasmes   cerogenes alaruasa   aphaena   pyrops

acrocinus longimanus   rosenbergia straussi

calloplophora sollie   jummos ruckeri

goliathus regius   goliathus orientalis   goliathus cacicus

cigales   acherontia atropos   anaea archidona

cithaeria   bhutanitis lidderdalei   anaxita constricta

brahmaea   caligo   caligo

acknowledgements The Fondation Cartier pour l'art contemporain would like to thank

The Hand of Nature
was displayed for the first time
at the Fondation Cartier pour l'art contemporain, in Paris,
as part of the exhibition *être nature*, in 1998.

Anne and Jacques Kerchache for their generosity and their loyalty.

Ettore Sottsass, who with great kindness and commitment immediately agreed to write a text for this book.

Larry Kazal, who with talent designed this book.

Patrick Gries, who photographed *The Hand of Nature* with enormous sensitivity.

Johanna Grawunder for her very valuable help.

And all those who were involved in this project: Vincent Beaurin, Aube Breton-Ellouet, Marine Degli,
Fabrice Domercq, Gilbert Lachaume, Grazia Quaroni, Sylvie and Marc Satore,
as well as Serge L'Estimé, Denis Simon and Jean-Pierre Galloudec, Analogue, Paris.

Curator of the Fondation Cartier pour l'art contemporain: Hervé Chandès

Secretary General: Nicolas Bos

Press Officer: Linda Jarton-Chenit

Editions of the Fondation Cartier pour l'art contemporain: Dorothée Charles

Design: Larry Kazal

The text by Jacques Kerchache was translated from French by Mark Hutchinson.

The text by Ettore Sottsass was translated from Italian by Marguerite Shore.

The book *The Hand of Nature* is published with the support of the Fondation Cartier pour l'art contemporain,
placed under the aegis of the Fondation de France, and with the sponsorship of Cartier.

First published in the United Kingdom in 2000
by Thames & Hudson Ltd, 181A High Holborn, London WC1V 7QX

First published in the United States of America in hardcover in 2000
by Thames & Hudson Inc., 500 Fifth Avenue, New York, New York 10110

Original French edition published by the Fondation Cartier pour l'art contemporain and Actes Sud

Photographic credits

© Patrick Gries for the Fondation Cartier pour l'art contemporain

Previous page: Philippe Chancel

Flyleaves:
Simone Breton in the studio, circa 1927, private collection/rights reserved.
André Breton, circa 1939, private collection/rights reserved.

© Jacques Kerchache

© Ettore Sottsass

© 2000 Fondation Cartier pour l'art contemporain and Thames & Hudson

British Library Cataloguing-in-Publication Data
A catalogue record for this book is available from the British Library
Library of Congress Catalog Card Number 00-100981

ISBN 0-500-97492-6

Printed and bound in France by Imprimerie Le Govic, Nantes